Sing a-ho that I
had the wings of a
dove;
I'd fly away
and be at rest.

—*slave spiritual*

Sewing Stories

HARRIET POWERS' Journey from Slave to Artist

BY
Barbara Herkert

ILLUSTRATED BY
Vanessa Brantley-Newton

ALFRED A. KNOPF · NEW YORK

Harriet Angeline Powers was born into slavery on October 29, 1837, according to Clarke County records. She was one of 5,000 African Americans in bondage in that county alone.

See that sweet baby
girl lying on a quilt her mama made?
What could she be dreaming of?

On a plantation near Athens, Georgia,
Harriet's mama worked from rise to set
while Harriet slept between the cotton rows.

Harriet grew up watching women carding cotton, spinning thread, dyeing and weaving cloth. She learned that wild indigo made blue, hickory bark made brown, and cherry bark made deep red. She studied strong, stained fingers. Her heart beat to the booming of the loom.

Slave women were involved in making textiles for the plantation. After they spun cotton into thread, they dyed it with natural coloring and wove it into cloth on a loom.

In the evening, the women gathered together and cut flour sacks and worn clothes into suns and moons and stars, lions, birds, and elephants for appliquéd cloth legends of Mother Africa. Harriet listened to their voices hum throughout the quarters, late into the night.

Some slave women sewed all day for the slaveholder's family. Only at night could they create for themselves. Appliqué is a technique where cut designs are stitched onto background fabric. The Master frowned on slaves staying up late to sew.

Most slaves were forbidden to learn to read and write. They passed on stories verbally and recorded them in cloth. Women sang and sewed by candle or pine-knot light in rough log cabins in a section of the plantation called the quarters.

Little Harriet placed cotton filling in the quilt. She held the pine-knot light high. "I won't nod off. No, ma'am." She was part of a sacred tribe. By a crumbling fireplace, in the middle of the night, Harriet learned to sew stories.

On Sundays and holidays, sometimes the Master gave permission for a quilting bee. The women lowered wooden frames from cabin rafters. Long-limbed Harriet crawled under those big frames and watched needles dart through cloth like silver dragonflies. She thought, "Someday I'm gonna sew a magic world."

While the Mistress of the plantation usually supervised the sewing, at a quilting bee the slave women could be their own artists, making designs with strips of cloth. For a few daylight hours, they might have felt free.

When the women finished sewing, making two or three quilts in just one day, folks gathered for peach pie and ginger cake, collard greens and barbecue. While they gobbled up the grub, Harriet traced quilted shapes with her finger. Her mama smiled. "Child, I think it's time you had a needle of your own."

"Yes, ma'am!"

The men were not allowed at the gathering until the quilting was over. Then they were invited in for a big meal, followed by a lively dance party. The women raised chickens and grew extra food in small gardens. They cooked in big, open fireplaces.

Strong-limbed Harriet helped the women sew. Afterwards, she danced at the frolic. Horsehair fiddles, cheese-box tambourines, and sheep-bone drums formed the band. If Armsted Powers could capture Harriet beneath a quilt, he could claim a hug and a kiss! Harriet slowed her pace, just a little bit. Sure enough, Armsted caught her with a story.

Young ladies gathered at the quilting bees as much to dance and flirt as to sew. They danced the Turkey Trot and the Mary Jane. Buckets, pans, and grass reeds were also used as musical instruments.

Harriet and Armsted jumped the broom together when Harriet was just eighteen. Soon Harriet became a mama; she named her pretty baby Amanda. "Pray we stay together and don't get sold away," she said.

Harriet wrapped Amanda in a quilt she made
and held her tight as Civil War cannons fired.

The army from the North marched into Athens. The Union soldiers told the slaves, "You're free."

"Hallelujah! Free at last!" Harriet cried.

But trouble didn't end with the war. Oh, no. Poverty raced through Georgia. How would Harriet feed her family? Amanda, Alonzo, Nancy, Lizzie, and baby Marshall— five hungry faces, ten bare feet. "Show me the way," Harriet prayed.

The Emancipation Proclamation declared the slaves free on New Year's Day, 1863. But it could not be enforced in areas still under rebellion. In Georgia, slaves were not freed until Union General Sherman's army invaded in 1864. Slaves in Athens were most likely emancipated sometime after the fall of Atlanta in September 1864.

In Athens, the aftermath of the war was worse than the war itself. Food, medicine, and clothing were scarce. Smallpox ravaged the town.

Harriet took up her needle, turning snips of calico and an old pair of dungarees into cloth stories that warmed her children and lifted her from hard times for a while.

"You gotta take what you've been given and make something out of it," she said.

In addition to making quilts, Harriet may have earned extra money by sewing clothes. Armsted earned very little as a farmhand.

Harriet saved every extra nickel. The family bought a little farm, a horse, a plow, and some seed. Now plates of catfish steamed on the table; fat vegetables ripened on the vine. The children grew, like the cotton Armsted planted. Cotton mills popped up all over Georgia, and folks celebrated good times.

Sometime in the 1880s, Harriet and Armsted bought four acres near Sandy Creek, outside of Atlanta. The family fished and grew vegetables, and profitable cotton. Cotton mills purchased cotton from local farmers like Armsted.

Athens announced its own party, the Cotton Fair. Folks were abuzz about the craft exhibit. Who would win Best in Show? "I reckon the good Lord gave me a skill," Harriet said. She snipped calico as pink as watermelon. She cut strips of cloth as green as Key limes.

Harriet sewed stories of Cain and Abel, Jacob and Jesus, too—familiar stories that formed pictures in her mind. She stitched Bible folks in scenes where polka-dotted camels, elephants, and ostriches lived together in a fabric land.

Harriet had grown up hearing Bible stories from the "chairbacker," a slave who proclaimed he'd been called to preach. She might have sat in the back at the slaveholder's church. She was fascinated by circus animals.

The Northeast Georgia Fair of 1886, called the Cotton Fair, included a Wild West show, several weddings, and a circus. Folks entering the craft exhibit competed for Best in Show, but Harriet was not reported as the winner.

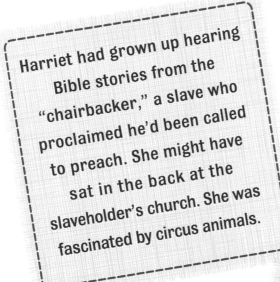

Folks at the Cotton Fair gathered around Harriet's quilt.
A young woman, Jennie Smith, offered to buy it.
How could Harriet part with a piece of her heart?
"No, ma'am. Not for any price."

Harriet hung her quilt in the corner of the exhibit tent, next to seed displays, jars of pickles, and mounds of potatoes. Jennie Smith, an art teacher, recognized it as a rare work of art.

Dark days came a-knocking when the price of cotton fell.
Harriet sent word: Would Miss Smith still like the quilt?
Oh, yes. Harriet climbed into an oxcart, and as Armsted
drove her into town, she cradled that quilt, like a child.

Harriet told Miss Smith, "You can have it for ten dollars."

"I only have five to give," Miss Smith replied.

"I reckon that'll do, owing to the hardness of the times."

Then Harriet explained each story sewn within the squares, like the lyrics of a song spun into cloth. She climbed back in that oxcart, and as Armsted drove away, her lap felt as empty as her heart.

Miss Smith wrote down Harriet's descriptions of the eleven panels of her creation. "It is my intention," Miss Smith wrote, "to exhibit this quilt in the Colored Building at the Cotton States Exposition in Atlanta."

Some Atlanta University faculty wives saw the first quilt at the exposition and commissioned the second quilt as a gift for the vice president of the board. This time, Harriet mixed Bible stories with local tales and legends she'd grown up hearing—the meteor shower of 1833 and Black Friday of 1780, when a combination of smoke from forest fires, a thick fog, and cloud cover caused an unusual darkening of the sky.

We don't know how much Harriet earned for the second quilt, but it attracted a lot of attention. In 1902, Atlanta University held a conference called The Negro Artisan. Harriet's quilt may have inspired the event.

Now folks were a-talking—could Harriet make another story quilt? Oh, yes. She pieced together Bible stories and tales of real events in the sky—a meteor shower, bright lights burning in the night. "It was snowing fire," Harriet said. "On a day called Black Friday, the sky grew dark as midnight, and all the cows and roosters went to bed."

Harriet delivered the quilt to some ladies in Atlanta, slipping their dollar bills into her apron pocket. Her heart was heavy—another beloved sold away. Still, it pleased her to hear the women's praise.

Harriet never had much money; she didn't own much property. It was a struggle to get by. Her cloth stories lifted her to another world, where suns and moons, animals and angels, danced together across a fabric sky. "One day shall I reach heaven, and one day shall I fly."

Harriet Powers died of pneumonia on January 1, 1910. Now everyone can see the world as she did, for her work hangs in two fine museums and is celebrated worldwide.

AUTHOR'S NOTE

Harriet Powers lived most of her life in poverty. Today her story quilts are priceless treasures. The first story quilt (the "Bible" quilt) resides at the National Museum of American History, part of the Smithsonian Institution, in Washington, D.C. The second, "Pictorial" quilt resides at the Museum of Fine Arts in Boston. No other quilts by Harriet are known to exist, although recent scholarship indicates she made at least five.

Harriet knew her quilts needed to be explained, and Jennie Smith had the foresight to record her words. A handwritten essay filled with Harriet's cloth stories and the circumstances of Jennie and Harriet's meeting was preserved with the first story quilt. Jennie invited Harriet to visit her "child" at any time, and apparently Harriet did on several occasions. We don't know who recorded the descriptions of the second story quilt.

Although she never traveled outside of Georgia and never went to a formal school, Harriet's artistic vision was vast. Jennie likened her style to that of the Impressionists. "I regret exceedingly that it is impossible to describe the gorgeous coloring of the work," she wrote. Harriet grew up surrounded by appliqué artisans and perpetuated this quilt-making technique into adulthood. Although the colors have faded, Harriet's art is an invitation into her thoughts, her life, and her dreams. Her story quilts lift us high.

ABOUT HARRIET'S PHOTOGRAPH

Harriet was photographed sometime in 1896 or 1897 at the professional studio of Charles F. McDannell in Athens, Georgia, wearing an apron decorated with appliquéd symbols of a cross and a sun. This photograph may have been taken when her quilt was exhibited. It is the only known photograph of Harriet, although another copy of it appeared in the collection of the Lee County Historical Society in Iowa.

BIBLIOGRAPHY

Fry, Gladys-Marie. *Stitched from the Soul: Slave Quilts from the Antebellum South*. Chapel Hill: University of North Carolina Press, 1990.

Hicks, Kyra E. *This I Accomplish: Harriet Powers' Bible Quilt and Other Pieces*. Arlington, Va.: Black Threads Press, 2009.

Killion, Ronald, and Charles Waller, eds. *Slavery Time When I Was Chillun Down on Marster's Plantation: Interviews with Georgia Slaves*. Savannah: Beehive Press, 1973.

Lyons, Mary E. *Stitching Stars: The Story Quilts of Harriet Powers*. New York: Charles Scribner's Sons, 1993.

Smithsonian Institution, Anon. n.d. Information Sheet on Harriet Powers Bible Quilt, T14713. Washington, D.C.: National Museum of American History, Textile Division.

Ulrich, Laurel Thatcher. "A Quilt Unlike Any Other: Rediscovering the Work of Harriet Powers." Work in Progress. Cambridge, Mass.: Harvard University, 2008.

Vlach, John Michael. *The Afro-American Tradition in Decorative Arts*. Athens: University of Georgia Press, 1990.

Wahlman, Maude Southwell. *Signs and Symbols: African Images in African American Quilts*. Atlanta: Tinwood Books, 2001.

EXPLANATION OF THE FIRST STORY QUILT

Described by Jennie Smith (from top, left to right)

1. Adam and Eve in the Garden of Eden, naming the animals and listening to the whispers of the serpent.

2. A continuation of paradise. Eve has given birth to a son, who has made a pet of a fowl. The bird of paradise is in the bottom right corner.

3. "Satan amidst the seven stars." The devil appears jaunty.

4. Cain is slaying his brother, Abel. Abel, being a shepherd, is accompanied by sheep.

5. Cain going into the Land of Nod. There are bears, leopards, elks, a "kangaroo hog," and a calico lion in the center, with a white tooth sticking from its lower lip.

6. Jacob lying on the ground with an angel ascending (or descending) the ladder to heaven.

7. The baptism of Christ, with "the Holy Spirit extending in the likeness of a dove."

8. The Crucifixion. The globular objects attached to the crosses represent the darkness over the earth.

9. Judas and the thirty pieces of silver. The large disk at his feet is the "star that appeared in 1886 for the first time in three hundred years."

10. The Last Supper, but the number of disciples is curtailed by five. Judas is clothed in drab.

11. Joseph, Mary, and the Infant Jesus with the Star of Bethlehem over his head.

HARRIET'S EXPLANATION OF THE SECOND STORY QUILT

(from top, left to right)

1. Job praying for his enemies. Job's crosses. Job's coffin.

2. The dark day of May 19, 1790. The seven stars were seen at noon. The cattle went to bed, the chickens to roost, and a trumpet was blown.

3. The serpent lifted up by Moses, and women bringing their children to be healed.

4. Adam and Eve in the Garden of Eden. Eve is tempted by the serpent.

5. John baptizing Christ, and the spirit of God descending and resting on his shoulder.

6. Jonah is cast overboard and swallowed by a whale.

7. God created two of every kind of animal, male and female.

8. The falling of the stars on November 13, 1833. People thought that the end of time had come.

9. Two of every kind of animal, continued. Camels, elephants, giraffes, lions, etc.

10. The angels of wrath and the seven vials. A seven-headed beast that rose out of the water.

11. Cold Thursday, February 10, 1895. A woman frozen at prayer. Another woman frozen at a gateway. A man frozen with a sack of meal. Icicles formed from the breath of a mule.

12. The red-light night of 1846. A man tolling the bell to notify the people of the wonder.

13. Bob Johnson and Kate Bell of Virginia, who told their parents to stop the clock at one and tomorrow it would strike one. The independent hog that ran 500 miles from Georgia to Virginia.

14. The creation of the animals continues.

15. The Crucifixion of Christ between two thieves.

To Jackie, for showing me the way.
And with thanks to Lauren Whitley, textiles
curator at the Museum of Fine Arts, Boston,
for her time and expertise.
—B.H.

To my mama, Shirley A. Brantley, who
taught me that I could always make
something from nothing.
Thank you, Mama. I love you.
And to the nine, and to Sharonda
Coleman Singleton and family.
—V.B.-N.

THIS IS A BORZOI BOOK PUBLISHED BY ALFRED A. KNOPF

Text copyright © 2015 by Barbara Herkert
Jacket art and interior illustrations copyright © 2015 by Vanessa Brantley-Newton

All rights reserved. Published in the United States by Alfred A. Knopf, an imprint of Random House
Children's Books, a division of Penguin Random House LLC, New York.

Knopf, Borzoi Books, and the colophon are registered trademarks of Penguin Random House LLC.

First story quilt copyright © National Museum of American History, Smithsonian Institute.
Second story quilt copyright © 2015 Museum of Fine Arts, Boston.

Visit us on the Web! rhcbooks.com

Educators and librarians, for a variety of teaching tools, visit us at RHTeachersLibrarians.com

Library of Congress Cataloging-in-Publication Data

Herkert, Barbara.
Sewing stories : Harriet Powers' journey from slave to artist / Barbara Herkert. — First edition.
p. cm.
ISBN 978-0-385-75462-0 (trade) — ISBN 978-0-385-75463-7 (lib. bdg.)
ISBN 978-0-385-75464-4 (ebook)
1. Powers, Harriet, 1837–1910—Biography—Juvenile literature. 2. African American
quiltmakers—Georgia—Juvenile literature. 3. African American quilts—Georgia—Juvenile literature.
4. African American women—Georgia—Juvenile literature. I. Title.
NK9112.H467 2013 746.46092—dc23 [B] 2013037480

The text of this book is set in 16-point Mrs Eaves. • The illustrations were created with
traditional gouache, Corel Painter 11, and Photoshop.

MANUFACTURED IN CHINA
December 2015
10 9 8 7 6 5 4 3
First Edition